Child Brides, Global Consequences

How to End Child Marriage

COUNCIL *on*
FOREIGN
RELATIONS

July 2014

Gayle Tzemach Lemmon
Lynn S. ElHarake

Child Brides,
Global Consequences
How to End Child Marriage

The Council on Foreign Relations (CFR) is an independent, nonpartisan membership organization, think tank, and publisher dedicated to being a resource for its members, government officials, business executives, journalists, educators and students, civic and religious leaders, and other interested citizens in order to help them better understand the world and the foreign policy choices facing the United States and other countries. Founded in 1921, CFR carries out its mission by maintaining a diverse membership, with special programs to promote interest and develop expertise in the next generation of foreign policy leaders; convening meetings at its headquarters in New York and in Washington, DC, and other cities where senior government officials, members of Congress, global leaders, and prominent thinkers come together with CFR members to discuss and debate major international issues; supporting a Studies Program that fosters independent research, enabling CFR scholars to produce articles, reports, and books and hold roundtables that analyze foreign policy issues and make concrete policy recommendations; publishing *Foreign Affairs*, the preeminent journal on international affairs and U.S. foreign policy; sponsoring Independent Task Forces that produce reports with both findings and policy prescriptions on the most important foreign policy topics; and providing up-to-date information and analysis about world events and American foreign policy on its website, CFR.org.

The Council on Foreign Relations takes no institutional positions on policy issues and has no affiliation with the U.S. government. All views expressed in its publications and on its website are the sole responsibility of the author or authors.

For further information about CFR or this paper, please write to the Council on Foreign Relations, 58 East 68th Street, New York, NY 10065, or call Communications at 212.434.9888. Visit CFR's website, www.cfr.org.

Contents

Foreword

Child marriage is a cultural practice that continues to harm the lives and limit the futures of millions of girls around the world. Ending the tradition is more than a moral imperative; research shows that early marriage results in reduced schooling, limiting girls' economic potential. It is also correlated with high rates of sexual violence and abuse, and with higher rates of maternal and infant mortality.

For several years, many nongovernmental organizations, such as The Elders and Girls Not Brides, have made ending child marriage a central goal. Recently, the ramifications of child marriage have begun to garner international attention among policymakers and governments. Through research, meetings, and publications, the Council on Foreign Relations has also worked to shed light on this challenging issue from a policy perspective. In May 2013, CFR Fellow for Women and Foreign Policy Rachel Vogelstein made the link between child marriage and broader strategic issues with her seminal report *Ending Child Marriage: How Elevating the Status of Girls Advances U.S. Foreign Policy Objectives.* Vogelstein's policy recommendations for how the United States might tackle child marriage have helped shape policymakers' conversation about ending the practice.

With generous support from the Ford Foundation, CFR Senior Fellow Gayle Tzemach Lemmon has deepened our understanding of child marriage with the two reports in this volume. "High Stakes for Young Lives: Examining Strategies to Stop Child Marriage," coauthored with Research Associate Lynn ElHarake, takes a close look at the social, economic, and cultural factors contributing to the practice to identify effective approaches to combat it—and where more data is needed. In "Fragile States, Fragile Lives: Child Marriage Amid Disaster and Conflict," Lemmon reviews an emerging body of research that suggests the practice is exacerbated during times of crisis as parents and families turn to child marriage to protect their daughters or alleviate heightened economic burdens.

Over the past year, the Women and Foreign Policy program has hosted a roundtable meeting series at CFR, bringing together leaders from the public, private, and nonprofit sectors to discuss how ending child marriage can drive social and economic progress. CFR also helped broaden the conversation about child marriage with its online InfoGuide, which offers an interactive, comprehensive look at this complex issue.

CFR's work builds on a growing consensus that curbing child marriage will allow U.S. investments to go further in supporting international development efforts, from education to health and human rights. These reports serve as a resource for policymakers who seek to develop a greater understanding of the causes of child marriage and implement strategies to eliminate the practice worldwide.

Isobel Coleman
Senior Fellow and Director, Women and Foreign Policy Program
Council on Foreign Relations
July 2014

Acknowledgments

For the past two years, CFR fellows in the Women and Foreign Policy program have prioritized elevating child marriage on the U.S. foreign policy agenda. This report is a part of those efforts, and was made possible by a generous grant from the Ford Foundation. The views expressed herein and any errors are my own. A special acknowledgment is extended to James M. Lindsay, CFR's director of studies, Isobel Coleman, director of CFR's Women and Foreign Policy program, and Rachel Vogelstein, a fellow in CFR's Women and Foreign Policy program. I would like to thank Lynn ElHarake, the research associate in CFR's Women and Foreign Policy program, for her support on this project. I am also grateful to Patricia Dorff, Ashley Bregman, and Eli Dvorkin for their review of previous drafts, and to Sigrid von Wendel, Grace Haidar, Shahrzad Mohtadi, and Rebecca Allen for their excellent assistance in the production of this paper. This report was published under the auspices of the Women and Foreign Policy program.

Gayle Tzemach Lemmon

High Stakes for Young Lives: Examining Strategies to Stop Child Marriage

Gayle Tzemach Lemmon
Lynn S. ElHarake

Introduction

"Only once I have settled down and gotten a job will I marry. There is a difference in generations; they have started educating girls because boys and girls are equal now.... I will be the first in my family to become a teacher; my parents do farming. That is why I want to make sure I have a job. I will help to take care of my parents."
—Sushma, age eighteen, India

"I do know some girls who had to drop out after twelfth class who were good at their studies. Their parents said they couldn't study any further. I felt bad and my mother also tried to encourage the girl, but her parents wouldn't allow it."
—Aryu, age eighteen, India

"I want to become a nurse; I am not thinking about a husband. My parents always told me to study and become successful."
—Seema, age nineteen, India

An estimated one-third of girls around the globe become brides before the age of eighteen and one in nine do so before the age of fifteen.[1] In recent decades, the issue of child marriage has grown in profile and priority for many policymakers. The Elders, a group of global leaders including former United Nations (UN) secretary-general Kofi Annan and former U.S. president Jimmy Carter, have taken on the issue and opted to use their platform to speak out against the practice, as have other prominent international organizations.[2] The UN estimated that in 2011, nearly seventy million women ages twenty to twenty-four had married before they turned eighteen.[3] If current trends continue without pause, in the next ten years, more than 140 million girls will be married before their eighteenth birthdays. In order to design interventions that can scale to match the level of the challenge, it is critical to understand the drivers of child marriage and the factors that can curb it.

Though global attention is new, the practice of child marriage—which also is called early marriage and forced marriage—is not. For centuries, it was the norm in societies spanning income levels and historical traditions. Policymakers define child marriage as either a formal or customary union in which one or both parties are under eighteen.

Child marriage harms women and girls: it is a practice that disrupts a child bride's educational and economic opportunities, raises her chances of exposure to violence and abuse, threatens her health and the health of her children, and ultimately hampers progress toward nearly every international development goal, including the Millennium Development Goals.[4] Child brides experience heightened exposure to sexual activity at an early age and an increased chance of early childbirth, both of which can have dire consequences on maternal and reproductive health, as well as on the health and well-being of their children. Young girls who are married before they complete their education often drop out of school, ending their educational opportunities and limiting their—and their families'—economic potential. Once married, girls and women face great challenges in entering the workforce, leaving them less able to contribute to household incomes and preventing them from helping to grow local economies. Moreover, child marriage is highly correlated with domestic and sexual violence, as girls who are married as children are more likely to be abused. Indeed, child marriage threatens the stability and economic progress of the communities in which child brides live and perpetuates the cycle of poverty in which so many poor countries find themselves trapped.

A mix of complex factors accounts for the slow pace of eliminating child marriage. Culture and tradition push to maintain the status quo, and the twin perils of poverty and lack of education also drive the practice. Lack of educational opportunity often limits girls' potential; combined with poverty, it makes child marriage an enduring reality. Yet, even as education and economic opportunities become more accessible overall, helping to alleviate poverty, countries where religious and traditional justifications for child marriage are deeply entrenched will not see an end to child marriage without shifts in social norms.

In many countries where child marriage occurs, laws ban the practice. But those laws often remain words on paper only, and are both unenforced and unheeded. Today, child marriage remains the norm in a number of regions around the world. In Niger, 75 percent of girls marry before the age of eighteen, and in India and Eritrea that figure is close to 50 percent.[5] As a recent post from the U.S. Agency for International Development (USAID) noted, "more than 40 percent of women marry before age eighteen in sixteen of the forty-seven countries surveyed, including three countries where more than 60 percent of women marry before age eighteen: Bangladesh, Guinea, and Mali."[6] Laws also can move in the opposite direction. For example, Iraqi law currently sets the legal marriage age at eighteen, but a current draft law under consideration could pave the way for brides as young as nine.

All of these factors mean that no one option provides an answer to the challenge of child marriage. Instead, a mix of legal frameworks, education policies, enforcement standards, attitude shifts, and economic incentives is required to ensure that the practice is eradicated in all communities, including those where it is a deep-rooted cultural practice.

U.S. policymakers have spoken out on the practice of child marriage at the international level and high-profile campaigns such as Girls Not Brides have highlighted the issue among global policy elites, as well as among the general public.[7] But despite the growing attention on child marriage, a solid understanding about what works and what does not work to combat the practice remains elusive. It is clear that laws alone have not changed the reality of girls' lives and the commonplace nature of the tradition. A number of nongovernmental organizations (NGOs) are working on different pieces of the policy puzzle and pressing on different levers to see what interventions make a difference in preventing child marriage and shifting attitudes about the tradition. Further research on the social, economic, and cultural factors that contribute to child marriage will help decrease, if not eventually eliminate, the practice.

Background

Over the past century, the age of marriage has risen in most countries, along with increased household incomes and greater access to education.[8] Yet, child marriage still exists in great numbers across the world and is particularly prevalent among rural and poor populations in developing countries. Though far less common, child marriage is still practiced in parts of the developed world, especially among immigrant populations. As one report from the United Kingdom noted, the number of British children "forced into marriage is hard to gauge," but 14 percent of calls to the country's Forced Marriage Unit's helpline in 2012 concerned the marriage of children under fifteen years old.[9]

The prevalence of child marriage transcends geographical and cultural boundaries, and it is not associated with any single religion or tradition.[10] The practice affects millions of girls annually: based on current rates of child marriages, some fourteen million girls this year—39,000 a day—will marry before they turn eighteen, and nearly half of these child brides will marry before they are fifteen.[11]

For almost a century, local programs and international initiatives have worked to reduce the incidence of child marriage. Organized efforts to curb the practice emerged as early as the 1920s.[12] One of the first legislative attempts to end child marriage occurred in India in 1929 with the passage of the Sarda Act.[13]

In recent decades, global gatherings such as the International Conference on Population and Development Programme of Action and the Beijing Declaration and Platform for Action have recognized child marriage as a human rights violation.[14] Many governments with persistently high rates of child marriage have committed to eradicating the practice by enforcing existing laws, raising the legal age of marriage, and increasing support for programs working to prevent and eliminate child marriage.[15] Yet, though child marriage overall is on a "downward trajectory, particularly among younger girls," child marriage rates have remained high in parts of sub-Saharan Africa and South Asia, particularly among the poorest citizens and in rural regions.[16]

INTERNATIONAL INITIATIVES

On the first International Day of the Girl Child on October 12, 2012, the United Nations called on leaders at the local, regional, and international levels to end child marriage. On September 25, 2013, the Human Rights Council, the leading UN body responsible for the promotion and protection of human rights around the world, adopted A/HRC/24/L.34, its first-ever resolution on child, early, and forced marriages.[17] The resolution, which calls on states to recognize "human rights obligations and commitments to prevent and eliminate the practice of child, early and forced marriage," received support from 107 countries around the world, including countries with some of the highest rates of child marriage: Ethiopia, South Sudan, Sierra Leone, Chad, Guatemala, Honduras, and Yemen.

Also in 2013, the fifty-seventh UN Commission on the Status of Women (CSW 57) featured a special session that focused on child marriage in support of UN secretary-general Ban Ki-Moon's Every Woman Every Child effort. The gathering ended with a commitment to "review, enact and strictly enforce laws and regulations concerning the minimum legal age of consent and the minimum age for marriage, raising the minimum age for marriage where necessary, and generate social support for the enforcement of these laws in order to end the practice of child, early and forced marriage."[18]

In determining the world's next set of development goals, the High-Level Panel of Eminent Persons on the Post-2015 Development Agenda proposed ending child marriage by 2030 as a specific milestone for its second goal to empower girls and women and achieve gender equality. "Child marriage is a global issue across, but sensitive to, culture, religions, ethnicity and countries," reads the report. "When children marry young, their education can be cut short, their risk of maternal mortality is higher and they can become trapped in poverty."[19] The panel's inclusion of child marriage as a goal in its report indicates a growing recognition that eliminating child marriage is not only a human rights issue, but one that limits the potential of communities and economies.

CHILD MARRIAGE AND U.S. POLICY

The Obama administration's development assistance funding in the 2014 fiscal year included $19 million to support initiatives that advance gender equality and the status of women and girls with the goal of promoting stability, peace, and development.[20] Because child marriage rates are an indicator of gender equality, reducing the practice globally should help the United States achieve foreign policy objectives that aim to raise the status of girls and women around the world, thereby promoting greater stability and prosperity.

In 2012, the Obama administration announced a strategy aimed at fighting violence against girls and women around the world that named child marriage as a violation of girls' and women's rights.[21] USAID also released a policy framework that offered policy recommendations for eliminating child marriage.[22] Additionally, in launching new public and private partnerships against child marriage, former secretary of state Hillary Clinton announced that the United States would begin requiring that the U.S. State Department's annual Country Reports on Human Rights Practice track each country's legal minimum age of marriage, as well as child marriage rates.[23]

Strategies for Ending Child Marriage

PROMOTING GIRLS' EDUCATION

In his message on the first International Day of the Girl Child, UN secretary-general Ban highlighted education as one of the most effective paths to curbing early marriage, stating, "Education for girls is one of the best strategies for protecting girls against child marriage. When they are able to stay in school and avoid being married early, girls can build a foundation for a better life for themselves and their families."

Several studies have examined the link between education and child marriage. A 2008 study of several West African countries using 1990s data and a recent study using 2006 data from Nigeria revealed that child marriage accounts for 15 to 20 percent of school dropouts.[24] Studies in Bangladesh concluded that each additional year of delay in age of marriage boosted schooling by 0.22 years and the likelihood of literacy by 5.6 percentage points.

Though further research is needed to understand more completely the relationship between child marriage and schooling, what is clear is that education increases women's economic opportunities. According to data from the World Bank, each additional year of education beyond the average boosts women's wages 10 to 20 percent.[25] Often marriage marks the end of schooling for young brides.[26] Studies show that girls with no education are three times more likely to marry or enter into a union before their eighteenth birthday than those who graduate from secondary school or higher.[27] Similarly, girls who complete only primary school are twice as likely to marry before their eighteenth birthday as their peers who obtain a secondary or higher degree.[28] In every region assessed in the United Nations Population Fund's (UNFPA) 2012 *Marrying Too Young* report, child marriage rates were higher for girls who did not reach secondary education levels.[29] The disparity was greatest in sub-Saharan Africa, where 66 percent of women with no education were married before age eighteen, compared to only 13 percent of those with secondary or higher education.[30]

In many cases, staying in school is a consequence of parents' decision to postpone age of marriage.[31] That decision also had positive spillover: First, when the girl was in school, she was more likely to be viewed by her parents as a child and thus not ready for marriage. Second, schooling allowed girls to meet others similarly interested in education and acquire social networks and skills that helped them to better communicate and negotiate their needs and desires.

The correlation between access to girls' education and reduced child marriage rates can be seen through the Berhane Hewan program in Ethiopia.[32] Ethiopia has one of the highest rates of child marriage in the world.[33] Launched with a pilot program in 2004, the Berhane Hewan program uses local strategies that protect young girls aged ten to nineteen from early and forced marriage in the Amhara region, where nearly half of girls are married before they turn eighteen.[34] The program also targets adolescent girls in the same age group who are already married or in unions.[35]

The program was pilot tested in Mosebo village in the Amhara region from 2004 to 2006, with a cohort from Enamirt village serving as the control group. Along with community outreach and awareness efforts, the Berhane Hewan pilot focused on encouraging girls to stay in school. The program offered options for girls in three different circumstances. Those who were still in school received materials, such as pens, notebooks, and readings, that supported their continued education. Those who had already left school but expressed interest in reenrolling received the same materials. And girls who had never attended school were placed in mentor-led groups that provided them with nonformal education, livelihood skills, and reproductive health education.

Prior to the program's launch, only 71 percent of all girls between the ages of ten and fourteen in the Berhane Hewan experimental group in Mosebo had ever been to school. By the end of 2006, 97 percent of girls in this cohort were attending school. Illiteracy also declined. About 45 percent of adolescent girls in Mosebo could not read at the start of the program, but that number fell to 21 percent by 2006. Additionally, average years of education rose. There was also significant improvement in the timing of marriage for children between the ages of ten and fourteen exposed to the program. These girls were 90 percent less likely to be married before age fifteen compared to their peers in the control group in Enamirt.[36]

ECONOMICALLY EMPOWERING
GIRLS AND WOMEN

Research shows that child marriage is concentrated in the world's poorest countries, and those countries with the lowest gross domestic product per capita usually have the highest child marriage rates.[37] Studies also show that household wealth may affect child marriage rates. An analysis by UNFPA found that more than half of girls in the poorest quintile of households assessed were child brides, more than three times the number in the wealthiest quintile of households. The report cited a "remarkable correspondence between lower rates of child marriage and characteristics commonly associated with higher levels of development such as urban residence, secondary or higher education and wealth."[38] South Asia shows the greatest wealth disparity, with women ages twenty to twenty-four in the poorest 20 percent four times more likely to be married before eighteen than those in the richest 20 percent.[39]

A combination of social, traditional, and economic pressures leads parents to marry their daughters off before they reach legal age. Many parents believe that finding a husband for their daughter secures her future, especially in times of social instability or fragility.[40] Daughters are sometimes also viewed as economic burdens or commodities. Additionally, child marriages can be a solution for mitigating familial or political disputes, or paying off debts, and customary requirements (e.g., dowries or bride prices) can also influence parents' decisions, especially in communities where families can give a lower dowry for young brides.[41] Finance-based programs encourage families to delay marrying their daughters. Loans, scholarships, subsidies, and conditional cash transfers (CCTs) are some of the most common incentives, and many focus on keeping girls in school. Other programs aim to give girls employment opportunities as alternatives to child marriage even beyond schooling. Incentives such as direct and unconditional cash transfers and income-generating activities can help provide girls with additional opportunities that raise their status in families and give them a say with parents and others to influence marital decisions. A World Bank pilot program in Malawi found that unconditional cash transfers led to reduced rates of teen pregnancy and early marriage and had the "effect of significantly delaying both."[42] Repeating this study in other countries and regions is critical to establish whether this approach could prove effective elsewhere.

INDIA: A CASE STUDY
ON ENDING CHILD MARRIAGE

CHILD MARRIAGE IN INDIA

South Asia has the highest rates of child marriage of any region in the world and India alone accounts for about 40 percent of the world's child brides.[43] As family incomes increase and more girls attend school in India, child marriage rates are going down, especially for younger girls. The rate of marriage for girls below the age of fifteen is declining more than twice as rapidly as for those marrying below eighteen.[44] But the percentage of women married before their eighteenth birthday remains high.[45]

A 2012 United Nations Children's Fund (UNICEF) report echoed UNFPA's results and found that the median age at marriage in India is inversely related to the household economic condition, with the country's poorest women marrying around five years earlier than women in the same age group in the wealthiest quintile.[46] The study also showed that women who had never been to school married at least three years earlier than their counterparts who had completed primary education.

APNI BETI, APNA DHAN: CONDITIONAL CASH TRANSFERS

The Indian government has taken steps to prevent child marriage.[47] The relationship between "son preference," education, economic status, and age at marriage, paired with the reality that laws alone do not change social norms, inspired the government of Haryana State to launch a CCT program in 1994 called Apni Beti, Apna Dhan (ABAD), meaning "our daughter, our wealth."[48]

The first of its kind in India, ABAD was a pioneer in testing the idea that a girl could be "revalued" with the help of economic incentives and financial products funded by the state. Implemented from 1994 to 1998 among the state's most disadvantaged families, it later was succeeded by a program called Ladli that was open to all parents, regardless of income.

Through a small payment at birth and a later conditional cash transfer if the daughter reached the age of eighteen unmarried, ABAD provided families with an incentive to embrace the idea of having a daughter, as well as to delay marriage by helping them to lighten other financial "burdens" associated with having a girl child, such as the cost of wedding clothes and jewelry. The program aimed to elevate the status of girls by reshaping perceptions of the value of daughters, traditionally viewed as burdens in Indian society, and was initially conceived as a way to change the country's skewed sex ratio.[49] In 1991, the sex ratio for the child population in Haryana (ages zero to six years) was 879 girls for every 1,000 boys.[50]

Through ABAD, the Haryana government gave mothers five hundred rupees (about eleven U.S. dollars) upon the birth of a daughter. Additionally, the government invested around 2,500 rupees in a savings bond under the girl's name. The initial cohort of ABAD participants, enrolled in 1994, reached their eighteenth birthdays in 2012, granting the first opportunity for program evaluators to assess the effectiveness of this program in delaying age of marriage.

SHIFTING SOCIAL NORMS

It is important to remember that ABAD addressed only one piece of the complex social ecosystem in which girls in India live. Between 1994 and 2014, much has changed. A push for greater awareness by the Indian government means that most families now know that the legal age of marriage in India is eighteen. In some cases, authorities intervene when underage marriage ceremonies are being conducted. In interviews with ABAD program participants, families cited weddings that were stopped because the bride was under the legal age of eighteen as one of the factors motivating them not to marry off their daughters.

Technology and access to schooling are also changing norms. The Internet and cellular phone technology have connected India to the world in ways that were unheard of only two decades ago. Access to social media, online Indian media, and global media content means modern and international influences are felt across India, including in rural regions.

Additionally, along with legal norms, enforcement, and technology, the trends regarding girls' education have been largely positive. The number of girls in school is rising and the gender gap in primary education has narrowed. Girls' enrollment at "both the primary and upper primary stages increased sharply" between 1990 and 2006.[51] Though parents remain more interested in their sons' educations than their daughters', girls' schooling is becoming increasingly accepted and embraced in many communities. The International Center for Research on Women (ICRW) found that more than two-thirds of Haryana's girls now are enrolled in secondary schools, compared to less than 50 percent in 2005.

Yet some recent changes have been far less promising for girls. In 2011, the Indian government census counted 830 girls (aged zero to six) for every 1,000 boys in Haryana, up from 820 a decade earlier, but still significantly lower than the 879 girls for every 1,000 boys counted in 1991.[52] Gender-biased sex selection and the skewed sex ratio in Haryana have an effect on girls' lives. In some communities, the scarcity of girls actually increases the risk that they will be subjected to violence, making some families even more likely to see marriage as a refuge that will guarantee their daughters' safety. As brides of marriage age become rarer, those few eligible girls who do remain in the community are increasingly vulnerable to rape and trafficking. These risks also make parents less willing to send their girls to secondary schools and colleges far from their home villages.[53]

It is against this evolving backdrop in India that the ABAD program unfolded. With funding from USAID, which wanted to understand the role of conditional cash transfers, ICRW is now completing its evaluation of the program. One of the earliest findings shows that the program has had a positive effect on girls' education. More girls who participated in the program stayed in school than those who did not. In its recent report, ICRW stated, "The girls who were beneficiaries attained higher levels of schooling, were more likely to continue their education and less likely to drop out than non-beneficiary girls, controlling for all other factors." Even though families did not receive the cash benefit until the girl turned eighteen, "the knowledge of the protracted benefit clearly influenced their decision to invest in their daughters' education. This is evident not only from the results on schooling but also some of the supplementary findings on the time girls get to study at home and the investment in sending them to a private school."[54]

In interviews with ABAD program beneficiaries, parents said that fewer girls in the community were getting married before age eighteen—though they did not always think this a positive development—and that many more people than in their generation sent their girls to school. Some fathers and mothers who had not completed their own secondary educations spoke about the importance of having their daughters complete school before being married: "Our parents didn't bother so much with our education," said one mother, Sarla, in an interview. "What I had to go through, I don't want my daughter to go through."

Interviews with girls and their parents included some families who said they had waited to marry their daughters until the girls reached age eighteen in order to receive the cash benefit.[55] Families used the ABAD money in a variety of ways. Some used it to cover the expense of wedding clothes and jewelry. A number of others, however, used the funds to cover school fees.

"Only once I have settled down and gotten a job will I marry," said Sushma, an eighteen-year-old woman enrolled in a basic training course for teachers. "I already spent my money on the course to become a teacher. . . . Girls I know are studying, but those who are married are not studying." Another young woman, Seema, used her ABAD money to enroll in a nursing course.

Additional evidence will be forthcoming as the ICRW study continues, and it will be important to see whether cash transfers, if shown to be effective, can be scaled in other locations where child marriage is prevalent in order to shape perceptions and practices that directly and indirectly affect the value families place on girls.

CHANGING COMMUNITY PERCEPTIONS AND BEHAVIOR

Although laws and economic incentives can help to make child marriage less attractive for families, they cannot on their own effectively end the practice and provide greater opportunities for all girls. For that, a broader and longer-term mindset evolution around the role of the girl is critical.

Interventions that use community-based behavior-change strategies can help to promote social change around the perception of girls and women, especially in countries that have yet to set a legal age of marriage.[56] In a review of child marriage programs, ICRW found that interventions that use behavior-change communications and community mobilization help to influence traditional perceptions and practices that "encourage or condone child marriage."[57]

These strategies acknowledge that girls rarely hold the power in their communities to decide when they marry, and that it is thus important to work with parents and community leaders—such as religious leaders and society elders—who make decisions on girls' behalf. Changing attitudes about child marriage is an especially critical intervention in communities where nonstate law dominates and where religious leaders often perform the marriage ceremonies.

A more comprehensive strategy will include programs working with religious leaders and educating men and boys on why delaying age of marriage is beneficial to all. Highlighting these two strategies is not meant to discount other interventions but rather to note two groups that are influential in deciding the future of girls and women in many communities.

RELIGIOUS AND CULTURAL LEADER INVOLVEMENT

In a 2007 review, ICRW found that religion was a significant factor associated with child marriage prevalence.[58] However, there was no *single* religion associated with the practice across countries; various religions had high rates of child marriage, depending on the country.

Because people look to culture and religion to justify child marriage, religious and traditional leaders can be uniquely effective in shifting social and cultural norms away from the practice. They can leverage their networks to lobby for legal reform and use their spiritual influence to encourage followers to change views about sensitive cultural norms, including child marriage.

WORKING WITH MEN AND BOYS

In order to shift attitudes toward child marriage, some initiatives have sought to involve men as decision-makers, and boys as future decision-makers, in awareness-raising and outreach campaigns. In many countries where child marriage remains the norm, men serve as the gatekeepers for the women in their families, with fathers, brothers, husbands, and other male figures making most household and communal decisions, often with input from religious leaders. Particularly in communities where child marriage is deeply rooted in religious and cultural traditions, these groups should be included in efforts to prevent and eliminate child marriage if the practice is to be eradicated in regions and among populations where it has proved harder to stop.

The USAID Vision for Action cites the critical role of men in curbing child marriage: "Interventions that involve fathers and religious and traditional leaders broaden understanding of the dangers of child marriage, and the long-term benefits of education and economic opportunities."[59] Notably, the Vision for Action also prioritizes the involvement of boys: "Equally important is reaching out to boys at a young age to encourage equitable gender attitudes and norms so that they can be allies in preventing child marriage and change agents within their communities."[60]

"SAFE AGE OF MARRIAGE" IN YEMEN: FOSTERING CHANGE IN SOCIAL NORMS[61]

In an effort to mitigate child marriage in Yemen—one of twenty "hot spot" countries—the Safe Age of Marriage program aimed to alter social norms and community attitudes around child marriage by improving community knowledge of dangers associated with the practice, strengthening local support for extending girls' education, and working closely with religious figures and community leaders.[62]

The program trained twenty male and twenty female volunteer community educators, including religious leaders and midwives—individuals already respected in the community—to conduct outreach educational activities. For example, the community educators were each responsible for organizing four awareness-raising sessions that employed various techniques, such as role-playing, poetry recitations, and small discussion groups, and held these in community spaces, including schools and mosques. The community educators also hosted monthly health clinics to address the reproductive health challenges associated with early marriage and childbearing, worked with schools to raise awareness of the social and health consequences associated with child marriage, and distributed printed materials and disseminated radio messages on the health and social consequences of the practice.

After one year of the Safe Age of Marriage project, the community educators had conducted more than 1,316 outreach initiatives reaching nearly 29,000 people. The results from the final survey found that there was an 18 percent increase in awareness in the community about the benefits of delaying marriage. There is evidence that the Safe Age of Marriage project helped avert early marriages and reduce child marriage rates, but it is still too early to see representative results of the program. Additionally, the Yemeni government requested that religious leaders include child marriage messages in their sermons and the community educators continued to mobilize support around girls' education. Due to its success, the program was scaled up to include two additional districts in Yemen and increase outreach to religious leaders and policymakers to push implementation of a law that prohibits marriage for girls under seventeen. Conservative religious leaders and clerics objected to the law, first passed in 2009, and it continues to be a topic of legislative conversation. The recent National Dialogue Conference in Yemen issued a proposal for the country's new constitution to make marriage before age eighteen illegal.[63] Even Islah, an influential Islamist party in Yemen that has opposed such legislation in the past, has stated that if the proposal goes through, it will not fight to have it repealed.[64]

STRENGTHENING LEGAL FRAMEWORKS

A number of international frameworks define the minimum age for marriage at eighteen and most countries around the world have laws in line with these agreements. Though laws alone will not end child marriage, in some places attitudes are shifting, as illustrated by the proposal from Yemen's recent National Dialogue Conference. Enforcement, however, often lags behind the laws on the books. Additionally, criminalization of child marriage is not always effective in preventing or eliminating the practice, since it can drive the practice further underground. Law enforcement officials and activists are also subject to violent repercussions in trying to prevent marriages, and few regulations exist to protect them from such retaliation.[65]

Yet despite the challenges, strategies for preventing and eliminating child marriages cannot be successful without clear and enforceable laws that are upheld by local governments. Child marriage laws can be incorporated into a number of other regulations implemented and enforced to protect against human rights violations, especially those guarding the rights of children and women. Such regulations include those that criminalize marital rape, gender-based violence, and violence against women; human trafficking and slavery laws; and ceremonies that require consent to marriage from both individuals.

Another tool available is the passage of laws mandating birth and marriage registration. Only half of children under five in developing countries are part of birth registries, with some regions such as eastern and southern Africa and South Asia seeing registration rates hovering at around a third of their populations.[66] Birth registration gives a child an official and permanent identity.[67] The government then has a record of the child and can track his or her age, thereby decreasing the child's vulnerability to practices that include child marriage.[68] By documenting the actual age of girls, law enforcement officials would be better able to stop child marriages and girls would be more aware of their own age and whether they can legally be married.

In Bangladesh, where child marriage prevalence is the highest in South Asia and one of the highest in the world, the government has been working with Plan International to implement online birth registration programs.[69] In 2006, only 10 percent of Bangladesh's population had birth documents. Today, the government estimates that number has climbed to more than 75 percent of the population. Findings from Plan International show that birth registration has helped to reduce child marriage in Bangladesh as the organization and its partners work with the government "to expedite a shift to online birth registration in its working areas so that certificates can no longer be falsified to show an underage girl as being above eighteen."[70]

Recommendations

Success in eliminating child marriage depends foremost on those countries where the practice remains highly prevalent and/or legal, as well as in communities in which the tradition is still socially acceptable. However, the United States—in concert with NGOs, UN agencies and other intergovernmental organizations, and the private sector—can play a catalytic role in curbing, and eventually ending, the practice of child marriage around the world by pursuing the following:

- *Better track dollars and focus on more in-depth evaluation processes.* With many child marriage programs still relatively new, there is limited data available to date that can point to statistical successes in child marriage prevention and elimination. The United States can help to fund additional evaluations on existing programs and require that analyses be regularly conducted on all U.S.-funded projects. The United States can also use its leverage with other international institutions and multilaterals to push for high standards of analysis.

- *Break out data on gender-related programs to separate dollars devoted specifically to curbing child marriage.* Currently, it is not possible to determine how much the United States, other governments, and international institutions are spending on programs aimed specifically at curbing and eliminating child marriage. Instead, funding for child marriage falls into broader pools focused on gender, education, or health-related issues. Eliminating this data gap to more clearly understand specific and targeted child marriage–related investments would help to identify where current dollars are going and to understand if further investments are necessary, or if current investments should be redirected to increase effectiveness and efficiency.

- *Focus on innovations and the role they can play in curbing child marriage.* The United States is currently studying the role of conditional cash transfers, such as in the ABAD case. More research should be conducted to better understand the strategies that help to extend girls' education into secondary school and the effect of additional education on child marriage. Specifically, improving understanding of both unconditional and conditional cash transfer programs in other contexts, in addition to ABAD, would be a great help in deciding whether to scale up such programs, and where to do so. Legal registries also offer opportunities for further study, addressing whether current successes should be repeated in other contexts and determining what should be done to help support government implementation of such registries. This evaluation should be conducted in coordination with other partners such as the World Bank and initiatives and NGOs focused on ending child marriage.

· *Include child marriage elimination and prevention priorities in diplomacy.* In addition to analyzing programs to curb child marriage, the United States should use its diplomatic leverage to encourage government leaders and policymakers in other countries to prioritize eliminating the practice, and to support them in doing so through policy advising and funding. The importance of ending child marriage in efforts to improve educational attainment, economic development, and social stability should be included in diplomatic conversations with high-prevalence countries. The issue should also be included in broader conversations around gender equality, educational access, maternal and child health, violence against women, and human trafficking—issues that undermine development progress.

· *Support efforts to address the root causes of child marriage.* The United States should deploy public-private partnerships and use diplomatic platforms to support civil society efforts aimed at changing local perceptions by working with community leaders, including elders and religious leaders, and men and boys. This would not necessarily entail additional funds, but instead involve spotlighting such efforts through public events and written assessments and evaluations of programs where the data shows results. The universal nature of child marriage should be highlighted, as should the fact that local leaders are often at the forefront of making change. Additionally, the United States should conduct more thorough and accurate analyses of child marriage intervention programs targeting the social and cultural drivers of the practice; this would allow the United States, other funders, and local leaders to determine which strategies to prioritize in community-based interventions that can be implemented within stronger legislative frameworks and alongside other interventions addressing economic drivers.

- *Target funding for programs in countries with high prevalence rates by proportion and absolute numbers.* The United States should focus its development investments in countries with the highest prevalence rates; this will help determine where effective interventions can make a difference and whether and how they can be scaled. A particular focus should be placed on countries where clear majorities of girls are wed before the age of fifteen, such as Niger and several others in the West Africa region, and on countries where large population size means scaling successful interventions could have a large and significant effect, such as India. Special attention should also be devoted to girls from the poorest and most rural regions, given their higher likelihood of being married before the age of eighteen.

Endnotes

1. International Center for Research on Women (ICRW), "Child Marriage Facts and Figures," http://www.icrw.org/child-marriage-facts-and-figures.
2. See the Elders, http://theelders.org/about.
3. Rachel Vogelstein, "Ending Child Marriage: How Elevating the Status of Girls Advances U.S. Foreign Policy Objectives," p. 3. Analysis based on data provided by the Statistics and Monitoring Section, Division of Policy and Strategy, UNICEF, January 2013.
4. United Nations, International Day of the Girl Child, "2012 Theme: Ending Child Marriage," http://www.un.org/en/events/girlchild/2012/theme.shtml; The Millennium Development Goals are eight international development goals adopted at the UN Millennium Summit in 2000, each with specific targets aimed at addressing extreme poverty. UN Secretary General, Millennium Project, "About Millennium Development Goals: What They Are," 2006, http://www.un.org/millenniumgoals.
5. Rachel Vogelstein, *Ending Child Marriage*, p. 5. Analysis based on data provided by the Statistics and Monitoring Section, Division of Policy and Strategy, UNICEF, January 2013.
6. United States Agency for International Development (USAID), "Women's Lives and Challenges," March 7, 2014, http://blog.dhsprogram.com.
7. See the Elders, http://theelders.org/child-marriage/what-are-elders-doing; http://www.girlsnotbrides.org.
8. Tracy Dennison and Sheilagh Ogilvie, "Does the European Marriage Pattern Explain Economic Growth?" CESifo Group Munich, CESifo Working Paper Series 4244, May 2013, http://www.iga.ucdavis.edu/Research/All-UC/conferences/huntington-2013/dennison_paper.
9. United Kingdom All-Party Parliamentary Group on Population, Development and Reproductive Health, "A Childhood Lost," November 2012, http://www.khubmarriage18.org/sites/default/files/165.pdf.
10. ICRW, "How to End Child Marriage," 2007, http://www.icrw.org/files/publications/How-to-End-Child-Marriage-Action-Strategies-for-Prevention-and-Protection-Brief.pdf.
11. World Health Organization, "Child Marriages: 39,000 Every Day," March 7, 2013, http://www.who.int/mediacentre/news/releases/2013/child_marriage_20130307/en.
12. ICRW, "Solutions to End Child Marriage," 2011.
13. Ibid, citing Sumita Mukherjee, "Using Legislative Assembly for Social Reform: the Sarda Act of 1929," *South Asia Research*, 26(3), November 2006.
14. See "Overview," UNFPA's International Conference on Population and Development, https://www.unfpa.org/public/icpd; "Beijing Declaration and Platform for Action," created and adopted during the Fourth World Conference on Women, September 1995, http://www.un.org/womenwatch/daw/beijing/platform.

15. Center for Reproductive Rights, "Child Marriage in South Asia," 2013, http://reproductiverights.org/sites/crr.civicactions.net/files/documents/ChildMarriage_BriefingPaper_Web.pdf.

16. Vogelstein, *Ending Child Marriage*, p. 3.; UNFPA, "Marrying Too Young: End Child Marriage UNFPA Fact Sheet," May 2012, http://unfpa.org/files/live/sites/unfpa/files/youngtowed/WhatIsChildMarriageFactSheet2_1.pdf.

17. United Nations General Assembly, Human Rights Council, "Strengthening efforts to prevent and eliminate child, early and forced marriage: Challenges, achievements, best practices and implementation gaps," 24th session, September 25, 2013, http://www.girlsnotbrides.org/wp-content/uploads/2013/10/HRC-resolution-on-child-early-and-forced-marriage-ENG.pdf.

18. United Nations Commission on the Status of Women, "Agreed Conclusions on the Elimination and Prevention of All Forms of Violence Against Women and Girls," 2013, p. 12, http://www.un.org/womenwatch/daw/csw/csw57/CSW57_Agreed_Conclusions_(CSW_report_excerpt).pdf.

19. United Nations, *A New Global Partnership: Eradicate Poverty and Transform Economies Through Sustainable Development*, 2013, http://www.post2015hlp.org/wp-content/uploads/2013/05/UN-Report.pdf.

20. U.S. Department of State, Foreign Operations, "Congressional Budget Justification," volume 2, Fiscal Year 2014, p. 112, http://www.state.gov/documents/organization/208290.pdf; The White House, Office of the Press Secretary, "Preventing and Responding to Violence Against Women and Girls Globally," Executive Order, August 10, 2012, http://www.whitehouse.gov/the-press-office/2012/08/10/executive-order-preventing-and-responding-violence-against-women-and-gir.

21. The White House, Office of the Press Secretary, "Preventing and Responding to Violence Against Women and Girls Globally," 2012.

22. USAID, *Ending Child Marriage & Meeting the Needs of Married Children: The USAID Vision for Action*, October 2012, http://pdf.usaid.gov/pdf_docs/PDACU300.pdf.

23. U.S. Department of State, "Secretary Clinton Launches New Public and Private Initiatives to Raise the Status of Girls," October 10, 2012, http://www.state.gov/s/gwi/rls/other/2012/198768.htm.

24. Minh Cong Nguyen and Quentin Wodon, "Child Marriage and Education: A Major Challenge," 2008, http://www.ungei.org/files/Child_Marriage_Edu_Note.pdf.

25. Gene B. Sperling, "A Global Education Fund: Toward a True Global Compact on Universal Education," Council on Foreign Relations, January 2009, http://www.cfr.org/education/global-education-fund-toward-true-global-compact-universal-education/p18051.

26. Save the Children, *State of the World's Mothers*, 2004.

27. UNFPA, "Marrying Too Young"; World Health Organization, "Child Marriages: 39,000 Every Day."

28. UNFPA, "Marrying Too Young," pp. 34–35. Data gathered from seventy-eight developing countries in which a Demographic and Health Survey or Multiple Indicators Clusters Survey was undertaken over the period from 2000 to 2011. These countries represent close to 60 percent of the population of all developing countries.

29. Ibid., Figure 9.

30. Ibid., p. 37.

31. These findings are the result of interviews in preparation for this paper.

32. Annabel S. Erulkar and Eunice M. Karei, "Evaluation of Berhane Hewan," Population Council, 2007, http://www.popcouncil.org/pdfs/Ethiopia_EvalBerhaneHewan.pdf.

33. A recent study surveying women in Ethiopia showed that 17 percent of respondents had married before age fifteen and 30 percent had married at ages fifteen to seventeen.

Annabel Eruklar, "Early Marriage, Marital Relations and Intimate Partner Violence in Ethiopia," Guttmacher Institute, volume 39, number 1, March 2013, http://www.guttmacher.org/pubs/journals/3900613.html.

34. The Berhane Hewan program is a joint initiative by the Ethiopia Ministry of Youth and Sport and the Amhara Regional Bureau of Youth and Sport.

35. UNFPA, "Marrying Too Young," p. 25.

36. Erulkar and Karei, "Evaluation of Berhane Hewan," p. 14.

37. ICRW, "Child Marriage and Poverty," 2006, http://www.icrw.org/files/images/Child-Marriage-Fact-Sheet-Poverty.pdf.

38. UNFPA, "Marrying Too Young," p. 35.

39. Ibid., p. 19. According to Demographic and Health Surveys (DHS), which provide much of the current country-level child marriage data.

40. Ibid., p. 12.

41. Sajeda Amin, "Programs to address child marriage: framing the problem," Population Council: Promoting Healthy, Safe, and Productive Transitions to Adulthood, no. 14, January 2011, http://www.popcouncil.org/pdfs/TABriefs/14_ChildMarriage.pdf.

42. World Bank Group, "Cash or Condition: Evidence from a Cash Transfer Experiment," March 2010, p. 23, https://openknowledge.worldbank.org/bitstream/handle/10986/3988/WPS5259.txt.

43. Anita Raj, Lotus McDougal, and Melanie L. A. Rusch, "Changes in Prevalence of Girl Child Marriage in South Asia," JAMA, 307(19): 2027–29, 2012.

44. UNFPA, "Marrying Too Young."

45. UNICEF, "Child Marriage in India," December 2012, http://www.unicef.in/documents/childmarriage.pdf.

46. Ibid., Figure 9, p. 14.

47. Vogelstein, Ending Child Marriage, p. 19.

48. See ICRW, "Evaluating the Power of Conditional Cash Transfers to Delay Marriage in India," http://www.icrw.org/where-we-work/evaluating-power-conditional-cash-transfers-ccts-delay-marriage-india.

49. The 1991 Census in India showed a sex ratio of 926 females for every thousand males.

50. Census of India 2001, "Sex Composition of the Population," chapter 6, p. 5, http://censusindia.gov.in/Data_Products/Library/Provisional_Population_Total_link/PDF_Links/chapter6.pdf .

51. A. K. Shiva Kumar and Preet Rustagi, "Elementary Education in India: Progress, Setbacks, and Challenges," Oxfam India, September 2010, http://www.oxfamindia.org/sites/default/files/III.%20Elementary%20Education%20in%20India-Progress,%20Setbacks,%20and%20Challenges.pdf.

52. Census of India 2011, http://censusindia.gov.in/2011-prov-results/prov_data_products_haryana.html; Census of India 2001, "Sex Composition of the Population," chapter 6, p. 5, http://censusindia.gov.in/Data_Products/Library/Provisional_Population_Total_link/PDF_Links/chapter6.pdf.

53. As noted in several interviews undertaken for this paper.

54. Priya Nanda, Nitin Datta, and Priya Das, "Impact on Marriage: Program Assessment of Conditional Cash Transfers," ICRW, March 2014, http://www.icrw.org/publications/impact-marriage-program-assessment-conditional-cash-transfers.

55. In November 2013, Gayle Tzemach Lemmon, a senior fellow at the Council on Foreign Relations, traveled to Haryana with ICRW to conduct field interviews girls and their families who had participated in ABAD.

56. Gambia, Equatorial Guinea, Saudi Arabia, and Yemen remain the only four countries with no enforceable law setting the minimum age of marriage. See Vogelstein, Ending Child Marriage, p. 10.

57. ICRW, "New Insights on Preventing Child Marriage: A Global Analysis of Factors and Programs," 2007.

58. Ibid.

59. USAID, *Ending Child Marriage & Meeting the Needs of Married Children: The USAID Vision for Action*, October 2012, http://pdf.usaid.gov/pdf_docs/PDACU300.pdf.

60. Ibid., p. 7.

61. The Safe Age of Marriage project was implemented by the Extending Service Delivery (ESD) Project, funded by USAID, partnered with the Basic Health Services (BHS) Project in Yemen and the Yemeni Women's Union (YWU). Together they implemented the Safe Age of Marriage program as part of Yemen's national campaign to reduce child and maternal mortality. USAID, "'Safe Age of Marriage' in Yemen: Fostering Change in Social Norms," http://www.esdproj.org/site/DocServer/ESD_Legacy_Child_Marriage.pdf?docID=3663.

62. UNICEF, *The State of the World's Children 2013*, statistical table 9: child protection, 2013, http://www.unicef.org/sowc2013/files/Table_9_Stat_Tables_SWCR2013_ENGLISH.pdf; USAID, "'Safe Age of Marriage' in Yemen." http://www.esdproj.org/site/DocServer/ESD_Legacy_Child_Marriage.pdf?docID=3663.

63. Christine Hauser, "Yemen Takes a Step Toward Law Ending Child Marriage," *New York Times*, January 23, 2014, http://thelede.blogs.nytimes.com/2014/01/23/yemen-takes-a-step-toward-law-ending-child-marriage.

64. Human Rights Watch, "Yemen: Start Moving on National Dialogue Proposals," February 10, 2014, https://www.hrw.org/news/2014/02/09/yemen-start-moving-national-dialogue-proposals.

65. Center for Reproductive Rights, "Child Marriage in South Asia," 2013, http://reproductiverights.org/sites/crr.civicactions.net/files/documents/ChildMarriage_BriefingPaper_Web.pdf.

66. UNICEF, "Birth Registration: Progress," January 2013, http://www.childinfo.org/birth_registration_progress.html.

67. UNICEF, "Child Protection from Violence, Exploitation and Abuse," January 13, 2014, http://www.unicef.org/protection/57929_58010.html.

68. Human Rights Council (A/HRC/19/L.24) highlights the importance of birth registration in ensuring the "promotion and protection of all human rights, civil, policy, economic, social and cultural rights, including the right to development." Human Rights Council A/HRC/19/L.24, "Birth registration and the right of everyone to recognition everywhere as a person before the law," adopted March 22, 2012, http://www.ohchr.org/EN/HRBodies/HRC/RegularSessions/Session19/Pages/ResDecStat.aspx.

69. Plan, "Child Marriage in Bangladesh: Findings from a National Survey," 2013, p. 28, http://plan-international.org/files/Asia/publications/national-survey-on-child-marriage-by-plan-bangladesh-and-icddr-b.

70. Ibid.

Fragile States, Fragile Lives: Child Marriage Amid Disaster and Conflict

Gayle Tzemach Lemmon

Introduction

For decades, child marriage has been viewed as an unfortunate but inevitable social ill. Few policymakers have considered its eradication feasible given how entrenched the practice is across the globe: one in three girls worldwide marry before the age of eighteen and one in nine girls marry before the age of fifteen.[1] The United Nations (UN) estimates that if current trends continue, in the next decade 142 million girls globally will become brides before they turn eighteen. The implications are dire: research shows that child marriage both reinforces poverty and makes it harder to escape. The practice has curtailed advancement on Millennium Development Goals Four and Five—which call for a two-thirds reduction in the under-five mortality rate and a three-fourths reduction in maternal deaths by 2015, respectively—and has undermined the goal of achieving universal primary education.[2]

The world's spotlight has recently turned to child marriage and campaigns to eradicate the practice have gained some momentum as the World Bank, UN, and other international organizations have embraced the centrality of women and girls to global development. Countries in which child marriage is most prevalent tend to be among the poorest and least stable. The practice is ubiquitous in communities where poverty is widespread; birth and death rates are high; and there are lower overall levels of education, health-care access, and employment.[3]

Curbing child marriage has become increasingly important to the global development discussion, but it is not yet central to the discussion about security and stability, especially when examining fragile states affected by conflict and/or natural disaster. Today, one-third of the world's poor live in fragile states, and the Organization for Economic Cooperation and Development (OECD) estimates that number could grow to one-half by 2018 and to nearly two-thirds by 2030.[4] As defined by the OECD, a fragile region "has weak capacity to carry out basic governance functions, and lacks the ability to develop

mutually constructive relations with society."[5] Similarly, the nongovernmental organization (NGO) World Vision describes fragile states
as "those where a government cannot or will not act on its responsibility to protect and fulfill the rights of the majority of the population,
particularly the most vulnerable," as well as those where "communities are under greater stress caused by natural disasters, acute and
slow onset emergencies, civil and political conflict and insecurity."[6]
Natural disaster and armed conflict destroy property; interrupt or
even halt economic activity; and divert resources away from health
care, education, and infrastructure.

Although the conversation about child marriage in fragile contexts
has yet to capture policymakers' attention, evidence suggests the relationship between the two merits further and close study: all but one of
the top ten countries with the highest child marriage prevalence rates is
on the OECD list of fragile states (see Table 1).[7]

Three of the ten countries leading the Fund for Peace's Failed States
Index have child marriage rates well above 50 percent.[8] And of the
bottom eleven countries on the United Nations Development Program's Human Development Index, nine have child marriage rates
above 40 percent.[9] Most countries with the highest prevalence rates of
child marriage also rank high on global indexes of vulnerability to natural disasters.[10]

As the world grows more connected, poverty becomes more visible,
and the issue of what happens to women and girls living in these fragile,
sometimes ungoverned, spaces becomes central to questions of development that go beyond those countries' borders. Child marriage does
not *cause* fragile states, but it does reinforce poverty, limit girls' education, stymie economic progress, and, as a result, contribute to regional
instability. In addition, the onset of natural disasters and/or armed conflict limits economic opportunities, weakens social institutions, and
increases the chance of sexual violence and assault targeting women
and girls. In such circumstances, young unmarried girls face increased
risks, and early marriage becomes a more palatable option for parents
and families looking to protect their girls.

But there is a wide gap in data that assesses the degree to which fragile contexts perpetuate child marriage; as a result, there is also a gap in
informed intervention. Part of the reason for the data gap is simple:
relief initiatives and humanitarian responses often overlook girls' sus-
ceptibility to the practice during vulnerable times for their families.

TABLE 1: LOW-INCOME AND LOWER-MIDDLE-INCOME FRAGILE STATES AS DEFINED BY THE OECD

Afghanistan	Liberia
Bangladesh	Malawi
Burundi	Marshall Islands
Cameroon	Federated States of Micronesia
Central African Republic	Myanmar
Chad	Nepal
Comoros	Niger
Republic of the Congo	Nigeria
Democratic Republic of the Congo	Pakistan
Côte d'Ivoire	Rwanda
Eritrea	Sierra Leone
Ethiopia	Solomon Islands
Georgia	Somalia
Guinea	South Sudan
Guinea-Bissau	Sri Lanka
Haiti	Sudan
Iraq	Timor-Leste
Kenya	Togo
Kiribati	West Bank and Gaza
Democratic Republic of Korea	Uganda
Kosovo	Republic of Yemen
Kyrgyz Republic	Zimbabwe

Source: OECD, *Fragile states 2013: Resource flows and trends in a shifting world*, 2013.

Providing urgent aid overrides conversations about which populations might be most vulnerable to child marriage and what that means to the larger quest for regional stability.[11]

Until now, most of the research on child marriage in fragile states has been collected by international NGOs—such as World Vision, Human Rights Watch, and Mercy Corps—and local organizations, UN agencies, and individual researchers on the frontlines of disaster and conflict. This is a start, but more work remains. Governments, multilateral organizations, and relief agencies should prioritize research during and immediately after natural disasters and conflicts to provide hard evidence about the relationship between child marriage and fragility. This data will help produce more effective and targeted interventions to assist the youngest and most at-risk members of communities in crisis, and improve the future prospects of all members of the next generation in some of the most challenging corners of the world. Armed with such data, those responsible for providing humanitarian and emergency aid can begin to tackle the complex web of safety risks, educational disruption, and limits to economic opportunity that combine to make child marriage a viable option for families struggling to survive.[12]

The Status of Women and Girls
in Fragile States

During periods of instability caused by natural disaster and conflict, the poorest and most vulnerable in society, particularly women and children, find themselves in even more precarious situations as livelihoods, homes, and social norms are upended.[13] A 2003 article in the *American Political Science Review* found that women and children bear a disproportionate brunt of the long-term effects of civil war.[14] For example, in the Democratic Republic of the Congo alone, 1.5 million children have been displaced by one of Africa's longest conflicts.[15] Natural disasters also disproportionately endanger women and girls, who account for a stunning 70 percent of the world's internally displaced population and more than half of the two hundred million affected each year by natural disasters.[16] An Oxfam Report on the impact of the 2004 Asia tsunami noted that women were the majority of those killed and were least able to recover from the disaster. In the Aceh Besar district of Indonesia, for example, 75 percent of those who died were women; this left a male-female ratio of 3:1 among the survivors. Some of the women who did survive found themselves in internally displaced persons (IDP) camps, facing heavy risks of violence and trafficking.[17] Results of a study conducted by the London School of Economics showed that in 141 countries analyzed, gender differences in loss of lives due to natural disasters were directly correlated with the economic and social rights of women in the countries before disaster struck; in places where gender rights were equal, the losses were far less lopsided.[18]

Women and girls in fragile states lag far behind their counterparts in more stable regions across a slew of human development indicators—from nutrition and access to health services to educational attainment and economic opportunities.[19] Recurring natural disasters, short- and long-term conflict, forced migration and displacement, and eroding economic stability leave women and girls further vulnerable to exploitation. And during times of increased resource scarcity, including during periods of crisis or conflict, girls tend to lose out in favor of investing limited resources in boys.

Drivers of Child Marriage in Fragile States: Poverty, Lack of Education, and Insecurity

Social upheaval and gender-based violence increase in times of disaster and conflict. In response, families often resort to child marriage as a way to protect the most vulnerable members of communities from threats—real or perceived. In its research examining child marriage in fragile states, World Vision found that "fear of rape and sexual violence, of unwanted premarital pregnancies, of family shame and dishonor, of homelessness and hunger or starvation were all reported by parents and children as legitimate reasons for early marriage."[20] Though more research is needed to determine the extent to which this vulnerability drives child marriage, existing research shows that many of the twenty-five countries home to the highest rates of early marriage—including Niger, Chad, Bangladesh, Guinea, and Central African Republic—are also frequently among those considered most vulnerable to natural disasters and most frequently found on indexes of failed states.

Even in countries where legal frameworks to protect women and children already exist, institutional breakdowns exacerbate the challenge of ending child marriage. In many of the areas where child marriage is most entrenched, customary law can trump formal law, particularly when a state's reach and influence collapse. In fragile states, justice systems often falter and lose legitimacy, resulting in a widened gap between formal laws, including those that set a minimum age of marriage, and customary laws or practices followed at the community level. For example, in Nigeria, a country increasingly destabilized by radical groups, even lawmakers have been recorded participating in child marriage: in 2010, Al Jazeera reported that Nigerian senator Sani Ahmed Yerima allegedly married a thirteen-year-old Egyptian girl.[21] The Nigerian Marriage Act sets the legal age of marriage without parental consent at twenty-one, but with parental consent, children can be married at any age.[22]

In another example, many refugees of the ongoing Syrian conflict have been unable to acquire the means or documents to officially register their marriages and instead look to religious leaders, elders, or sheikhs to conduct marriage ceremonies. The resulting marriage contracts are not recognized by any state authority and therefore leave women and their children vulnerable, especially in times of divorce or separation.[23] Somalia, another conflict-ridden country, has set a legal minimum age of marriage at eighteen for girls. Yet weak enforcement by the government, entrenched tradition, and the forced marriage of girls by insurgency groups has left the country with one of the highest child marriage prevalence rates in the world.[24]

Communities may look to customary laws and traditions to use child marriage as a way to protect young girls, ignoring laws against the practice that may be viewed as irrelevant in times of instability.[25] Weak penalties and lax or nonexistent enforcement also allow communities to disregard formal laws.

RISE IN POVERTY AND LOSS OF ECONOMIC OPPORTUNITIES

Studies show that countries with the lowest gross domestic product (GDP) per capita are among those with the highest child marriage prevalence rates.[26] Of the ten countries with the lowest GDP in 2013, six—Malawi, Niger, Madagascar, Ethiopia, Central African Republic, and Guinea—fall among the top twenty countries with the highest rates of child marriage in the world.[27] Of the twenty-five countries with the lowest GDP, twelve have child marriage rates above 40 percent.[28] Household wealth is also thought to affect child marriage rates: an analysis by the United Nations Population Fund (UNFPA) found that more than half of girls in the poorest quintile of households assessed were child brides, more than three times the number in the wealthiest quintile of households.[29]

Fragile states buffeted by war and natural disaster find themselves struggling against the subsequent poverty that accompanies such upheavals. A comprehensive report on fragile states from the African Development Bank noted that "for every three years a country is affected by major violence, poverty reduction lags behind by 2.7 percentage points." Conflict can move previously comfortable families into lower income percentiles and make child marriage look like a promising option for their daughters' futures.

Parents and families turn to child marriage as a means of alleviating the economic burden of the girl, a burden that is increased during times of social instability and economic uncertainty. For example, in parts of rural Niger, United Nations Children's Fund (UNICEF) officials report that families use child marriage as a survival strategy during times of drought, accepting offers from men of wealth requesting to marry their daughters in the hopes that doing so will allow them to better care for other children. In countries facing high food insecurity and/or drought, such as Bangladesh and Somalia, girls and women are discharged from the household, while male children are seen as more valuable household assets.[30] Similarly in Uganda, food crises associated with climate change have forced young girls into "famine marriages" as they are exchanged for dowry or bride price.[31] UNICEF reports that in Liberia and Sierra Leone, parents have coerced their daughters into marriages due to economic destitution and violence in refugee camps.[32]

BARRIERS TO GIRLS' EDUCATION

In its 2012 report "Marrying Too Young," the UNFPA noted that girls with no education are three times more likely to marry or enter into a union before their eighteenth birthday than those who graduate from secondary school or higher. Girls who only complete primary school are two times more likely to marry or enter into a union than their peers who obtain a secondary or higher degree.[33] According to a UNICEF study, 36 percent of women in Senegal who did not attend primary school were married by the age of eighteen. In Tanzania, women who completed secondary school were 92 percent less likely to be married by eighteen than their peers who had attended only primary school. In Bangladesh, delaying marriage by one year increased the likelihood of literacy by almost six percentage points and kept a girl in school for longer. Moreover, research in several West African countries reveals that child marriage in Nigeria accounts for 15 to 20 percent of school dropouts.[34] In the Borno region of Nigeria, for example, the stronghold for the radical group Boko Haram, 37 percent of girls are married by age fifteen and the median age at first marriage is fourteen—the youngest in the country.[35] Likely due to regional instability, cultural traditions, and high rates of child marriage, less than 20 percent of girls aged fifteen to nineteen in Borno are literate.

Though education systems typically suffer overall during times of social instability, crises tend to impair girls' educational opportunities more than boys'. Girls enrolled in schools in fragile states are often forced to drop out and those who were already excluded may face even smaller chances of ever entering a classroom. For example, in Tajikistan, girls of school age who live in conflict-affected regions are less likely to complete their studies than girls in more stable areas; data shows that "exposure to violent conflict had a large and statistically significant negative effect on the enrollment of girls."[36] The same is observed after natural disasters. For instance, according to data gathered in Bangladesh—which has one of the highest child marriage rates in the world—following Cyclone Sidr in 2007, 62 percent of the total number of children under eighteen who were married in the five years before the study were married within the first year following the disaster.[37] The government of Bangladesh found that it was common for those adolescent girls who had lost an academic year of school due to the cyclone's wreckage to be forced into marriages.[38] In Kenya, gender, education, and global poverty-reduction initiatives found that increased poverty due to drought reduced school attendance and girls were more likely to be withdrawn from school than boys.[39]

Anecdotal evidence and interviews with NGO leaders running programs on the ground suggest that even in fragile times, education can be used to help mitigate the risk of child marriage. Schooling in emergency programs can be a strong protection strategy, especially when children are at risk of being trafficked or coerced into an armed group, prostitution, or marriage. Additionally, relief agencies have emphasized that schools should only be used as emergency shelters if all other options have been exhausted, in order to minimize disruption to education and further protect children. When using schools is unavoidable, alternative locations should be found as soon as possible.[40]

Conflict can also make girls' trips to and from school more dangerous, so parents and families keep them home from school to ensure their security. These girls may end up in marriages earlier than they would have if they could have safely attended school because parents see marriage as an additional safeguard against violence. However, though marriage protects the girl from attack on her way to school, it also limits her educational and economic opportunity. The Group of

Eight (G8) highlighted this risk in April 2013 in its Declaration on Preventing Sexual Violence in Conflict.[41]

INSECURITY AND VIOLENCE

The World Bank has noted that "rates of early marriage and teen pregnancy tend to be particularly high in insecure environments," which may be a manifestation of high levels of gender-based violence and/or parents' and guardians' desires to protect girls and help ensure their economic survival.[42] In a submission to the United Nations Office of the High Commissioner on Human Rights (UNHCR), the network Women Living Under Muslim Law noted that countries home to ongoing civil conflict show symptoms of child-related social stress, including "rising numbers of children on the streets, very young laborers, increasing child slavery and trafficking (including sexual slavery and trafficking), and high levels of child neglect and abandonment."[43] Experts estimate that in 2013, nearly thirty million children in conflict-affected nations were subjected to such violence or abuse by the time they reached age eighteen.[44]

In hopes of protecting their children from such harm, some parents and guardians turn to child marriage. A Save the Children study cites "increasing reports of early marriage as parents take desperate measures to 'protect' their daughters from sexual violence."[45] In Afghanistan, representatives of the organization Women for Afghan Women, which runs a series of shelters across the country, report: "We see families marrying off children when insecurity is increasing. People are afraid of what might happen to unmarried girls in the family. They are afraid of rape or kidnappings. Most people prefer for the girls to be married so that they are safe in their husband's house."[46] In Sri Lanka, another conflict-affected country, children have reportedly been forced into marriages to avoid being abducted and/or recruited by terrorist groups.[47]

Fear of violence also increases early marriage in the wake of natural disasters. For example, Oxfam noted a rise in child marriage following the 2004 Asia tsunami.[48] Although some of these marriages had been arranged before the tsunami, Oxfam noted that girls who lost both their parents were being married off by members of the extended family or the community to other young men and that the marriages "seem[ed] to be contracted in desperation and without involving the girls' consent."[49] As one young girl in Bangladesh told interviewers from Plan International, "After cyclones, families think their condition is worse and send their daughters to get married. Almost 50 percent of girls drop out of education because of early marriage. In very remote villages, it is probably more [like] 70 to 75 percent."[50] Similarly, Plan International found that early marriage increased following the 2010 floods in Pakistan and the earthquake in Haiti. In both locations, fear of sexual violence was thought to cause the increase.[51]

More data is needed to offer a true picture of the scope and drivers of child marriage in all fragile states. In a recent report by the International Displacement Monitoring Center, which examined the effects of violence and conflict in displacing young girls from their homes, the center argues: "Reliable and comprehensive data should be collected, disaggregated by sex and age, and [cover] IDPs both in camps and those living with host families and communities. This is essential in establishing a clear picture of boys' and girls' needs in terms of protection, education, shelter and basic and social services. Data on separated and unaccompanied children is needed to identify those most likely to suffer abuse and neglect."[52]

COUNTRY EXAMPLE: SYRIA

Syria is an example of how armed conflict can harm the lives of family members and young women. The number of children suffering from violence, displacement, and disease has soared and continues to rise in the ongoing conflict. Current approximations suggest that more than half of the estimated 2.8 million Syrian refugees are under the age of eighteen, and three-quarters of those are under the age of twelve.[53] Prior to the conflict, more than 95 percent of Syrian children were enrolled in primary school. But as refugees, only a small proportion of Syrian children have returned to the classroom. In Jordan, only about half of Syrian refugee children are in school and in Lebanon that figure is estimated at less than 20 percent.[54]

Sexual violence in Syria has been documented as a weapon of war used "to intimidate parties to the conflict destroying identity, dignity and the social fabrics of families and communities."[55] As detailed in accounts from refugees, women and girls cite the fear of rape as one of the main reasons for fleeing Syria.[56] But sexual violence has gone largely undocumented given social stigma and barriers to appropriate psychosocial and medical resources.[57] It is also the reason cited for many child marriages. In the case of Syria, interviews with refugees point to marriages that may have been arranged to "save the honor" of girls who have survived rape or who may be perceived to have been raped.[58]

There is strong indication that child marriage is increasing due to the conflict as well. A report from the United Nations noted that though early marriage occurred in Syria's rural communities prior to the 2011 start of the war, the lack of employment opportunities and family resources has led even more families to turn to early marriage for their girls.[59] The charity Mercy Corps reports anecdotal stories among refugee families with few resources about the rising the pressure on children to marry given the continuing instability and families' diminished prospects. Twenty percent of registered marriages of Syrian refugee women in Jordan involve a bride less than eighteen years of age. Though child marriage rates are difficult to document in the ongoing conflict, such estimates point to an increase from Syria's 11 percent child marriage figure provided by the Population Reference Bureau in 2001.[60]

Reports from refugee camps in Jordan also highlight the increased likelihood of young girls marrying much older men, believing that these men can provide financial "protection and stability."[61] A growing number of Syrian girls are reportedly married off in order to generate income for their poor refugee families.[62]

Recommendations

During periods of conflict and natural disaster recovery, girls and women face an especially complicated web of challenges. A breakdown in infrastructure and governance leaves girls vulnerable to social norms that, even when designed to protect them, in practice deprive girls of educational and economic opportunities and threaten their health and safety. Furthermore, U.S. foreign policy and development goals are undermined by child marriage; research consistently shows that progress toward educational attainment, improved health, and increased security are all hindered in communities where child marriage occurs.

Child marriage is more than a violation of human rights. It is a practice that undermines global development goals and U.S. foreign policy priorities. By exacerbating poverty, cutting short education, and limiting the economic possibilities for girls and women, the practice hinders the opportunity to increase global prosperity and stability.

Existing data and an abundance of qualitative evidence point to intensified risks of child marriage in fragile states affected by natural disaster, conflict, and other causes of social instability. A better understanding of the drivers of child marriage in such areas could lead to strong and effective intervention strategies that could curb and eventually eliminate the practice, helping to improve girls' futures and bring stability to their communities.

Given the educational, health, economic, and security benefits of combatting child marriage, more research is needed to bridge the existing data gaps, as well as smarter investments and heightened attention. Therefore, at critical times of disaster, conflict, and upheaval, the impetus to keep children in school and girls out of marriage when possible should be prioritized. Host governments, UN agencies, multilateral organizations, and domestic and international NGOs employing programs and strategies to keep girls in school, increase employment opportunities, and promote legislative frameworks should continue to uphold and implement such initiatives to the extent possible in response to natural disasters or conflicts. Working closely with such institutions, the U.S. government can spearhead and support efforts to curb child marriage in fragile societies affected by natural disaster and conflict by taking the following steps:

- *Collect reliable, consistent, and comprehensive data, disaggregated by gender and age, to provide a detailed understanding of the needs and risks of those affected by disaster and conflict, including refugees and internally displaced people.* Better data will allow for better development and implementation of solutions that address the drivers of child marriage more broadly.

- *Elevate the issue of child marriage in U.S. diplomacy and interactions with multilateral organizations and international NGOs to ensure that the health, educational, and economic needs of girls are not forgotten during periods of disaster and conflict.* This includes keeping the issue of child marriage at the policy fore during post-disaster and conflict aid and relief efforts, and also addressing tendencies for increased sexual violence against girls and women during times of fragility.

- *Immediately integrate the unique needs of girls into post-disaster and post-conflict planning.* This step includes making education a top priority and facilitating the creation of girls' schools and facilities near camps and other areas to which girls' families have fled. One such opportunity could involve investigating and implementing innovative programs that are thought to help keep girls in school and/or reduce child marriage in non-fragile states—such as unconditional or conditional cash transfers targeted specifically at girl children, as well as programs that give families some of the income they might have received if the girl were working or married.

Endnotes

1. UNFPA, "Marrying Too Young: End Child Marriage," 2012, http://unfpa.org/endchildmarriage.
2. World Health Organization, "Child Marriages: 39,000 Every Day," March 7, 2013, http://www.who.int/mediacentre/news/releases/2013/child_marriage_20130307/en/.
3. See UNFPA, "Marrying Too Young" and Rachel Vogelstein, *Ending Child Marriage: How Elevating the Status of Girls Advances U.S. Foreign Policy Objectives*, Council on Foreign Relations, May 2013.
4. OECD, "Fragile States 2014: Domestic Revenue Mobilisation in Fragile States," 2014, p. 15, http://www.oecd.org/dac/incaf/FSR-2014.pdf.
5. OECD, "Fragile States 2013: Resource Flows and Trends in a Shifting World," 2013, http://www.oecd.org/dac/incaf/FragileStates2013.pdf.
6. World Vision, "Untying the Knot: Exploring Early Marriage in Fragile States," p. 6.
7. This list of fragile states has been adopted from the OECD list of fragile states used in its report "Fragile States 2013." For this paper, only lower-income and lower-middle-income fragile states were included. The full list used by the OECD in the report is a World Bank-African Development Bank-Asian Development Bank harmonized list of fragile and post-conflict countries for the year 2012, http://siteresources.worldbank.org/EXTLICUS/Resources/FCS_List_FY12_External_List.pdf; 2011 Failed State Index, http://www.fundforpeace.org/global/library/fs-11-11-fsi-public-spreadsheet-2011-1107b.xls; World Bank income classification (August 2012), http://data.worldbank.org/about/country-classifications.
8. Fund for Peace, "The Failed States Index 2013," http://ffp.statesindex.org/rankings-2013-sortable.
9. UNDP, "Table 1: Human Development Index and its components," 2012, https://data.undp.org/dataset/Table-1-Human-Development-Index-and-its-components/wxub-qc5k.
10. World Vision, "Untying the Knot."
11. United Nations, "Gender, Humanitarian Assistance and Conflict Resolution," 1999, http://www.un.org/womenwatch/daw/csw/Mcaskie.htm.
12. World Vision, "Untying the Knot," Figure 1, p. 10.
13. Lorna Read, "Disengaged from Development: Fragile States and Vulnerable Populations," North-South Institute, December 12, 2012, https://www.nsi-ins.ca/newsroom/disengaged-from-development-fragile-states-and-vulnerable-populations/.
14. Hazem Adam Ghobarah, Paul Huth, and Bruce Russett, "Civil Wars Kill and Maim People—Long after the Shooting Stops," *American Political Science Review,* Vol. 97, No. 2, pp.189–202, May 2003, http://www.uky.edu/~clthyn2/PS439G/readings/ghobarah_et_al_2003.pdf.
15. "Democratic Republic of the Congo - UNICEF Humanitarian Action for Children 2014," ReliefWeb, February 21, 2014, http://reliefweb.int/report/

democratic-republic-congo/democratic-republic-congo-unicef-humanitarian-action-children-2014.

16. Internal Displacement Monitoring Center (IDMC) and the Norwegian Refugee Council, "Briefing Paper: Girl, disrupted," March 7, 2014, http://reliefweb.int/sites/reliefweb.int/files/resources/201403-global-girl-disrupted-brief-en.pdf.

17. UNFPA, "Gender-Based Violence in Indonesia: A Case Study," 2005, pp. 11–12, http://www.unfpa.org/women/docs/gbv_indonesia.pdf.

18. Eric Neumayer and Thomas Plumper, "The Gendered Nature of Natural Disasters: The Impact of Catastrophic Events on the Gender Gap in Life Expectancy, 1981–2002," *Annals of the Association of American Geographers*, 97(3), 2007, pp. 551–566, http://www.lse.ac.uk/geographyAndEnvironment/whosWho/profiles/neumayer/pdf/Disastersarticle.pdf.

19. United Nations, "Gender, Humanitarian Assistance and Conflict Resolution."

20. World Vision, "Untying the Knot," p. 8.

21. Al Jazeera, "Nigerian senator marries girl of 13," May 18, 2010, http://www.aljazeera.com/news/africa/2010/05/2010518858453672.html.

22. International Center for Nigerian Law, "Marriage Act, Chapter 218, Laws of the Federation of Nigeria 1990," http://www.nigeria-law.org/Marriage%20Act.htm.

23. Dominique Soguel, "For Syrian Refugees, Early Marriages End Early," Women's eNews, February 19, 2014, http://womensenews.org/story/marriagedivorce/140218/syrian-refugees-early-marriages-end-early#.U3DtDPldXzg.

24. Human Rights Watch, "No Place for Children: Child Recruitment, Forced Marriage and Attacks on Schools in Somalia," 2012, http://www.hrw.org/sites/default/files/reports/somalia0212ForUpload_0.pdf.

25. Plan International, "Weathering the Storm: Adolescent Girls and Climate Change," June 2011, p. 19, http://plan-international.org/about-plan/resources/publications/emergencies/weathering-the-storm-adolescent-girls-and-climate-change.

26. UNFPA, "Marrying Too Young," p. 35.

27. Based on rankings provided by ICRW. See http://www.icrw.org/child-marriage-facts-and-figures.

28. Data reviews time period from 2009 to 2013. World Bank, "World Development Indicators: GDP per capita," http://data.worldbank.org/indicator/NY.GDP.PCAP.CD/countries/1W?display=default.

29. UNFPA, "Marrying Too Young," p. 19. Data is according to USAID-sponsored Demographic and Health Surveys (DHS), which provide much of the current country-level child marriage data.

30. World Vision, "Untying the Knot," p. 24.

31. Plan International, "Weathering the Storm," p. 19.

32. UNICEF, "Impact of Conflict on Girls in West and Central Africa Region," 2005.

33. UNFPA, "Marrying Too Young," pp. 34–35. Data gathered from seventy-eight developing countries in which a DHS or Multiple Indicators Clusters Survey was undertaken over the period 2000 to 2011. These countries represent close to 60 percent of the population of all developing countries.

34. Minh Cong Nguyen and Quentin Wodon, "Child Marriage and Education: A Major Challenge," 2008, http://www.ungei.org/files/Child_Marriage_Edu_Note.pdf.

35. Nigeria Demographic and Health Survey, 2008.

36. Olga Shemyakina, "The Effect of Armed Conflict on Accumulation of Schooling: Results from Tajikistan," *Journal of Development Economics*, 95(2), May 2006, pp. 186–200.

37. World Vision, "Untying the Knot," p. 25.

38. Government of Bangladesh, "Climate Change, Gender and Vulnerable Groups in Bangladesh," Climate Change Cell, Department of Environment, Bangladesh, 2011.

39. Deen Thalif, "'Famine Marriages' Just one By-Product of Climate Change," Inter Press Service, March 9, 2010, http://www.globalissues.org/news/2010/03/09/4798.

40. IDMC and the Norwegian Refugee Council, "Briefing Paper: Girl, disrupted."

41. Lisa Davis, "Seeking Accountability and Effective Response for Gender-Based Violence Against Syrian Women: Women's Inclusion in Peace Processes," MADRE, March 21, 2013, http://www.peacewomen.org/portal_resources_resource.php?id=1983.

42. The World Bank, "Girls' Education in the 21st Century," 2008, http://siteresources.worldbank.org/EDUCATION/Resources/278200-1099079877269/547664-1099080014368/DID_Girls_edu.pdf.

43. Maggie Black, "Growing Up Alone: The Hidden Cost of Poverty," UNICEF UK, as quoted and cited in Women Living Under Muslim Laws, "Child, Early and Forced Marriage: A Multi-Country Study," December 15, 2013.

44. Save the Children, "Unspeakable Crimes Against Children: Sexual Violence in Conflict," 2013, http://www.savethechildren.net/sites/default/files/libraries/Unspeakable%20Crimes%20report.pdf.

45. Ibid., p. 6.

46. These findings are the result of interviews conducted with Women for Afghan Women on May 19, 2014.

47. Rose Wijeyesekera, "Assessing the Validity of Child Marriages Contracted During the War: A Challenge in Post-War Sri Lanka," Annual Research Symposium, University of Colombo, 2011, http://www.cmb.ac.lk/?page_id=2782.

48. Ibid., p. 19.

49. Oxfam International, "The Tsunami's Impact on Women," Oxfam Briefing Note, March 2005, http://www.preventionweb.net/files/1502_bn050326tsunamiwomen.pdf.

50. Plan International, "Weathering the Storm: Adolescent girls and climate change," p. 19.

51. Ibid., p. 19.

52. IDMC and the Norwegian Refugee Council, "Briefing Paper: Girl, Disrupted."

53. UNHCR, "Syria Regional Refugee Response," http://data.unhcr.org/syrianrefugees/regional.php.

54. UNICEF, World Vision, UNHCR and Save the Children, "Syria Crisis: Education Interrupted," December 2013, http://www.unicef.org/media/files/Education_Interrupted_Dec_2013.pdf.

55. Lisa Davis, "Seeking Accountability," p. 23.

56. Ibid., p. 10.

57. Ibid., p. 8.

58. UN Women, "Gender-Based Violence and Child Protection Among Syrian Refugees in Jordan, With a Focus on Early Marriage," 2013, as quoted and cited in Lisa Davis, "Seeking Accountability," p. 12.

59. UN Women, "Gender-Based Violence and Child Protection Among Syrian Refugees in Jordan, with a Focus on Early Marriage," 2013, http://www.unwomen.org/~/media/Headquarters/Attachments/Sections/Library/Publications/2013/7/Report-web%20pdf.pdf.

60. Hoda Rashad et al., "Marriage in the Arab World," Population Reference Bureau, 2005, http://www.prb.org/pdf05/marriageinarabworld_eng.pdf.

61. Lisa Davis, "Seeking Accountability," p. 12.

62. Sheera Frenkel, "Teenage Syrian Girls Are Being Sold Into Forced Marriages To Save Their Families," BuzzFeed, May 20, 2014, http://www.buzzfeed.com/sheerafrenkel/young-syrian-girls-are-being-sold-into-forced-marriages-to-s.

About the Authors

Gayle Tzemach Lemmon is the *New York Times* best-selling author of *The Dressmaker of Khair Khana* and a senior fellow with the Women and Foreign Policy program at the Council on Foreign Relations (CFR). Prior to joining CFR, Lemmon covered public policy and emerging markets for the global investment firm PIMCO, after working for nearly a decade as a journalist with the ABC News political unit and *This Week with George Stephanopoulos*. Lemmon has reported on entrepreneurs in conflict and post-conflict regions for the *Financial Times, New York Times, International Herald Tribune, Daily Beast, Fast Company, Politico, Huffington Post*, and Bloomberg. She is also the author of the *Newsweek* March 2011 cover story "The Hillary Doctrine" on former secretary of state Hillary Clinton's push to put women at the center of U.S. foreign policy. She has written regularly for the *Atlantic, Foreign Policy*, and *Foreign Affairs*. Lemmon appears frequently on news outlets including NBC News, National Public Radio, MSNBC, and CNN. Lemmon earned a BA in journalism summa cum laude from the University of Missouri School of Journalism and an MBA from Harvard Business School, where she received the 2006 Dean's Award for her work on women's entrepreneurship.

Lynn S. ElHarake is a research associate in the Women and Foreign Policy program at the Council on Foreign Relations. Prior to joining CFR, ElHarake worked for Global Health Strategies, a communications and advocacy consulting firm. There, she oversaw outreach to the Middle East and North Africa region, and also consulted directly for Women Deliver, a global advocacy nongovernmental organization, in the lead-up to its third global conference. She also worked as a research assistant to Iman Nuwayhid, dean of the faculty of health sciences at the American University of Beirut. She was a Fulbright scholar in Kuala

Terengganu, Malaysia. She has written for CFR blogs and other international development websites on issues related to women, the Middle East, and entrepreneurship. ElHarake graduated cum laude from Duke University with a BA in biological anthropology and Asian and Middle Eastern studies.